HOW TO
AVOID SHIPWRECK

Copyright 1986
Revised Edition 1991
MARK T. BARCLAY
PUBLICATION
All Rights Reserved

ISBN 0-944802-09-5

Cover Design
Heart Art & Design
501 George St.
Midland, MI 48640

HOW TO AVOID SHIPWRECK

Table of Contents

DEDICATION

I dedicate this book to Dr. John Osteen, one of the greatest heroes of the New Testament church, as well as one of the sharpest pastors, strongest missionaries and hardest fighters I know, whose momentum has set a pace for my life and ministry, as well as untold thousands of other hard-fighting ministers of the Gospel.

I salute you in the Lord, Pastor Osteen. Your courageous, overcoming spirit will never be forgotten. Thanks for the supreme Bible example you and Dodie have been to us.

You are giants of integrity to our Lord Jesus Christ!

CHAPTER 1

SHIPWRECK IN THE FAITH

"This charge I commit unto thee, son Timothy, according to the prophecies which went before on thee, that thou by them mightest war a good warfare;

Holding faith, and a good conscience; which some having put away concerning faith have made shipwreck."

1 Timothy 1:18-19

It is an awesome thing that is happening in the land today. Many, many people, both helpers and leaders, are wiping out. They are causing themselves destruction and disaster. Many people are giving in to sinful lusts and desires. Others are harboring anger, bitterness or hurts which cause their hearts to be troubled. How is it that so many people are giving in to sin? How is it that so many are discouraged, quitting their work and retreating to their homes? It's an awesome thing to see. I hope you will never be a part of it.

1

Why? Why all this trouble? Why are so many falling away? Why are so many quitting?

Paul (a seasoned apostle) wrote to Timothy (a young pastor) and charged him to war a good warfare. Timothy was instructed to remember the prophecies and the directions of the Lord for his life. Evidently, Paul was concerned about his welfare or the welfare of his followers. Both letters from Paul to Timothy are filled with warnings, instructions and guidelines of how to deal with troubled people, troubled times and the leadership of the church.

Notice in the verse we quoted earlier that two major areas were mentioned for Timothy to hold on to. He was told to hold on to these two things: faith and a good conscience. Paul warned him that if he let these two things go, he could go shipwreck like others had. If he would hold on to them, he would survive.

HOLDING FAITH

Many people have misunderstood what this means. Many have misused the faith. Holding on to faith means more than holding on to your belief or trust in God. It does include this kind of faith, but it always refers to our Christian walk as a whole. The faith is Christianity.

Holding on to faith is holding on to Christianity. I don't know why so many people think they can serve God any way they want to. You cannot! You can serve God only the way He tells you to. That's it!

There are no variations, no special exemptions or partialities. We cannot stop doing the proper principles and practices that are described by God and think we will still be pleasing to Him. We must be humble, holy, pure in motives and obedient to the Word of God and the great Holy Spirit.

Some people have put the faith away, and they have chosen to go shipwreck. "Put away" means that they have purposed to set it aside or cover it up or hide it in the background. No one can take your faith away from you. If you lose it, you put it away from yourself! I am talking about being disciples. I am referring to everyday Christian practices such as Bible study, prayer, church attendance, tithing, etc. Many people seem to think they can serve God without doing these things or doing them only partially. NOT TRUE!

God rewards those who diligently seek Him. If we seek first His Kingdom and His righteousness, we will be blessed and rewarded. And if we don't? WE WON'T BE! It's that simple!

People think they can read their Bibles little or not at all and still be strong in the Lord. WRONG! People think they can pray very little and still be strong in the Lord. WRONG! People think they can cheat God and the church on their finances and still be strong in the Lord. WRONG! People think they can stay home from church or survive on TV church alone and still be strong in the Lord. WRONG!

These kinds of people are headed for a horrible shipwreck. Now, they probably won't admit it, but I tell you, they are going to wreck. With some, it's just a matter of time!

A GOOD CONSCIENCE

This really is one of the most stabilizing forces we have. When our conscience is good, it aids greatly in keeping our attitudes proper. A good conscience helps to ground us in the faith. A good conscience beats off condemnation and guilt from us. A good conscience aids in leading us out of evil and keeps us doing good.

Paul said that some have put away their good conscience and have gone shipwreck in the faith. These people think they can get away with anything. They begin to sin willfully and expect God's blessing to just keep coming. They think they can play in immorality and abuse drugs and alcohol and still be blessed of the Lord. THEY ARE WRONG! DEAD WRONG!

Preachers all over the world are trying to be "man of the hour" with faith and power and still play with sin. You preachers that are playing with the toys and sin of lustful flesh had better repent quickly. If you don't, it will cost you your lives. You preachers who are fellowshipping with alcohol and drugs and pornography had better repent. You are walking down Death Row right now. You have put away (smothered) your good conscience, and it is deadly to live that way. Some have played around so long that their consciences have been seared as with a hot iron. It is dead and no longer sensitive to God. How sad! How sick!

A man's conscience can convict him of his wrong if it hasn't been put away from him, if he hasn't buried it under his lustful practices. (Read John 8:7-9.)

Paul wrote to the Corinthian Church and taught them about people who were in idolatry because of a weak conscience. (Read 1 Corinthians 8:7.)

Look, believer, whether you are a leader or a follower doesn't matter. You must hold on to the practice of good Christian sacraments, and you must let your good conscience aid you in right living. Put away these two, and we will watch you go shipwreck.

I don't understand some people. I've watched them, even in the church I pastor. They come and do all the practices of a good Christian. They pray, read their Bibles, worship, pay tithes and sit smiling through the sermon. They even shout an "amen" once in a while. They truly are holding on to faith, but they have put away a good conscience. This is the part that I don't understand about them. They'll do one without the other. I've watched them. With all their ability, they serve the Lord in church, and yet they still go shipwreck. Why? Because they play in sin. They work hard for God, but they play in sin. Some are in sexual immorality, others are in pornography, others are into financial idolatry and others are in lusts and worldly pleasures. They end up going shipwreck. No one can serve two masters. You either serve God, or you turn on Him and serve flesh. Believers that live like this need to repent – fast! Remember, no one has to end up in a shipwreck situation. Hold on to your faith and a good conscience, and you will never be left desolate!

If you will practice all the basic Bible practices of Christianity, you will surely be saved from horrible shipwreck. Be sure to pray, read your Bible constantly, be a true worshipper, pay tithes, be a forgiver and guard your heart and mouth with diligence. You'll see that God will help you through.

CHAPTER 2

SOFT, SOUTHERLY WINDS

"And when it was determined that we should sail into Italy, they delivered Paul and certain other prisoners unto one named Julius, a centurion of Augustus' band."

"Now when much time was spent, and when sailing was now dangerous, because the fast was now already past, Paul admonished them,

And said unto them, Sirs, I perceive that this voyage will be with hurt and much damage, not only of the lading and ship, but also of our lives.

Nevertheless the centurion believed the master and the owner of the ship, more than those things which were spoken by Paul."

"And when the south wind blew softly, supposing that they had obtained their purpose, loosing thence, they sailed close by Crete.

6

But not long after there arose against it a tempestuous wind, called Euroclydon.

And when the ship was caught, and could not bear up into the wind, we let her drive."

"And we being exceedingly tossed with a tempest, the next day they lightened the ship;

And the third day we cast out with our own hands the tackling of the ship.

And when neither sun nor stars in many days appeared, and no small tempest lay on us, all hope that we should be saved was then taken away."

"Then fearing lest we should have fallen upon rocks, they cast four anchors out of the stern, and wished for the day."

(Portions from Acts 27)

This is the account of the shipwreck that the Apostle Paul went through. We understand that it was an actual physical ship that wrecked in that storm. We also understand that many things can be learned here about us, and truth can be applied to our lives. Let's look a little closer.

It's amazing how well pastors and other ministry gifts can feel danger coming on. I have witnessed this with the flock that I pastor, both in individual lives and with the church as a whole. Just like Paul, I can perceive when shipwreck is drawing nigh.

7

But also, like Paul's situation, people usually listen to someone else besides the pastor or man of God. They listened to the ship's owner in Paul's case. They should have listened to Paul. Many people would save themselves hours, days and months of agony if they would only take heed to their pastor's heart-cry.

Let me talk to you for a moment about soft, southerly winds. In Paul's case, we read how the wind began to blow softly. It looked like the sailing conditions were perfect. It looked like it was the perfect time to step out and go. The only problem was that they didn't listen to Paul. They followed these soft, southerly winds, but not too long after they set sail, a horrible hurricane hit them.

This reminds me of people who are so anxious to get into their own ministries. They say things like, "Pastor doesn't recognize the anointing on my life," or "My ministry isn't received here," or "I feel called to get out on my own." It isn't long after this that the devil blows their way with a soft, tempting wind. Oh, yes, it looks like perfect sailing conditions. Sure, it looks like the perfect time to get out into their own ministries. It feels just like what they've been praying and waiting for.

Remember why Paul's shipmates wanted to sail? Because they didn't think the harbor they were docked in was good enough to hold them for the winter. Some people are just like this. They don't think their church is good enough to winter in. How sad!

Well, these people (tossed to and fro by every wind) take off and go out into their own ministries. Even when Pastor says, "No," away they go. Oh, they look great for a while, but just wait. Hey, anybody looks good in soft, southerly winds.

HOW TO AVOID SHIPWRECK

It isn't long, and the horrible, treacherous storms of life blow upon these free-sailing vessels. Do you know what happens next? They begin to unload cargo. That's right. Some unload their anointing, some unload their spouses and/ or children, others their self-esteem, and on and on. It's a miserable, sad sight to see, and it's usually because they didn't listen to their pastor.

Well, what about other people? What about those who do listen and follow leadership? What do they do in the midst of the storms of life?

There is a beautiful truth to be found here in this record of Paul's shipwreck. The truth fits all kinds of people, and no matter why the storms of life blow upon you, you can be saved by the truths. Let me quote Acts 27:29.

> *"Then fearing lest we should have fallen upon rocks, they cast four anchors out of the stern, and wished for the day."*

This is what you and I can do in the midst of our storms. We can anchor our souls and our lives. We can stop the storm from beating our ships to pieces. In every storm there are two choices for boatmen to make: (1) Be driven by the wind, and (2) Anchor your vessel. The best thing to do is to anchor your vessel and wait for the storm to pass over.

Listen, my friend, you and I don't always know what lies in wait for us. We don't always know what kind of storm is about to blow in on us. We don't always know all the snares the devil has set for us.

Be wise. Be strong. Prepare yourself for these storms. Listen to good leadership. Hear from God on the issues of your life, and don't be led by those soft, southerly winds.

CHAPTER 3

ANCHORING THE SOUL

"Which hope we have as an anchor of the soul, both sure and stedfast, and which entereth into that within the veil;

Whither the forerunner is for us entered, even Jesus, made an high priest for ever after the order of Melchisedec."

Hebrews 6:19-20

It goes without saying that Jesus is the anchor of our souls. It is Jesus who has purchased us with His blood and who has been made Head of the church. If we are rooted and grounded in Him, we will grow up and be fruitful, productive people. Everyone who knows Jesus knows this truth. (Read Ephesians 3:17-18.)

"As ye have therefore received Christ Jesus the Lord, so walk ye in Him:

HOW TO AVOID SHIPWRECK

Rooted and built up in him, and stablished in the faith, as ye have been taught, abounding therein with thanksgiving.

Beware lest any man spoil you through philosophy and vain deceit, after the tradition of men, after the rudiments of the world, and not after Christ."

Colossians 2:6-8

It is our responsibility to keep our souls anchored in Christ. There are a lot of things that will try to draw us away from Christ, but we must remain in Him. There are a lot of opportunities to go and to do, but not all opportunities are of God.

It would be glorious to think that every Christian everywhere was settled into Christ and totally committed to the church. This, however, is far from being accurate. Many Christians pull up their anchors and are bashed into the rocks or run their ships aground. (Read Acts 27:40-41.)

Look at some of the scriptures that alert us to the happenings of the times in which we live.

"Now the Spirit speaketh expressly, that in the latter times some shall depart from the faith, giving heed to seducing spirits, and doctrines of devils;

Speaking lies in hypocrisy; having their conscience seared with a hot iron;

Forbidding to marry, and commanding to abstain from meats ..."

"... refuse profane and old wives' fables, and exercise thyself rather unto godliness."

(Portions from 1 Timothy 4)

"Some men's sins are open beforehand, going before to judgment; and some men they follow after.

Likewise also the good works of some are manifest beforehand; and they that are otherwise cannot be hid."

1 Timothy 5:24-25

"This know also, that in the last days perilous times shall come.

For men shall be lovers of their own selves, covetous, boasters, proud, blasphemers, disobedient to parents, unthankful, unholy,

Without natural affection, trucebreakers, false accusers, incontinent, fierce, despisers of those that are good,

Traitors, heady, highminded, lovers of pleasures more than lovers of God;

Having a form of godliness, but denying the power thereof: from such turn away.

For of this sort are they which creep into houses, and lead captive silly women laden with sins, led away with divers lusts,

Ever learning, and never able to come to the knowledge of the truth."

"... so do these also resist the truth: men of corrupt minds, reprobate concerning the faith.

But they shall proceed no further: for their folly shall be manifest unto all men, as theirs also was."

(Portions from 2 Timothy 3)

One could meditate in these scriptures all day long. It is sad and even a little nauseating to think that some Christians will be this way instead of being Christ-like, but I have witnessed this with my own eyes, and I am sure that you have also.

"Help us, Lord Jesus, to stay rooted and grounded in You, growing up and flourishing as Your disciples."

I feel so sorry for people who leave their church and abandon their pastor and their brothers and sisters. These people need our prayers, for they are about to go severely shipwreck in the faith. They have uprooted themselves. They have ungrounded their stance in God. What a shame. What a waste of Godly potential.

"For the time will come when they will not endure sound doctrine; but after their own lusts shall they heap to themselves teachers, having itching ears;

13

*And they shall turn away their ears from the
truth, and shall be turned unto fables."*

2 Timothy 4:3-4

I say to this kind of people, "Anchor your souls in Jesus.
Go back to your pastor and go back to your local church and
make things right. How long do you think you can last playing
this game? Go back! Make things right! Reground yourselves in Christ!"

Some people think they love Jesus and only want to make
a silent, hidden commitment to Him in their hearts. I tell you,
you will not last. The commitment to Jesus starts in the heart,
but it must include discipline and Christian sacraments and
practice. You can't be a hearer only, or you will deceive
yourself. You must be a doer of the Word.

Every believer must prove himself and prove his own
work according to the scriptures. You must be a faithful
steward and a dependable servant of the Lord.

The devil has lied to so many people. He has told them that
it is easier to do their own thing. He has convinced many
people to do what they want to do and say what they want to
say.

Every Christian everywhere knows that the devil is a liar.
He lies to us. He is out to deceive us and cause us to uproot
ourselves and go out on our own. His oldest trick is to isolate
you from the rest of the Body of Christ.

Shake yourself. Shake off the enemy. Put off self-
centeredness and selfish ways. Ground yourself in Christ.
Anchor your soul in Him. Find root in Jesus. Set your
affection on the things that are above.

CHAPTER 4

PRAYER – AN ANCHOR TO THE SOUL

*"But in a great house there are not only
vessels of gold and of silver, but also of
wood and of earth; and some to honour, and
some to dishonour.*

*If a man therefore purge himself from these,
he shall be a vessel unto honour, sanctified,
and meet for the master's use, and prepared
unto every good work."*

2 Timothy 2:20-21

We all have the same chance to be vessels of honor. Some
people think there is no choice. They say that God has
predestined some to honor and some to dishonor. This only
displays their lack of understanding.

The Lord's house is a great house. In every great house
there are vessels of honor and dishonor. This includes the
house of the Lord, but vessels of honor have no guarantee
that they will stay this way. In the same way, vessels of

dishonor do not have to stay dishonorable. This is the beauty of God. When we are displeasing to God, we can change. We all have the same chance to do good. Don't blame God for your bad condition or bad attitude. It is not God doing this to you. You can change and become a vessel of honor. Look closer at verse twenty-one. It says:

"If a man therefore purge himself from these, he shall be a vessel unto honour ..."

There it is! Did you see it? The difference between vessels of honor and vessels of dishonor is purging. He who purges himself becomes a vessel of honor.

Listen, God isn't going to miraculously deliver you from rebellion or dead works or miserable attitudes or sinful practices. You have to go to prayer and purge yourself of these.

Remember we talked about Paul's shipwreck? When they could no longer continue on their voyage safely, they threw four anchors out of the stern of the ship and waited for daylight to come upon them.

This is what you have to do, believer. You have to pick up this great anchor of prayer and put it to work for you. You have to do this yourself. It is your duty to purge yourself in prayer.

Quit blaming others for your miserable life. People seem to blame their spouses, their parents, their pastors, their churches, their friends and so on. Blame yourself! It's nobody's fault but yours!

HOW TO AVOID SHIPWRECK

Go to God in prayer. Repent of your wicked ways and your bad attitudes. Confess your sins. Admit you have been arrogant and rebellious. You can purge yourself and, once again, become a vessel of honor.

Please don't be found on the list of those who turn from the truth. I pray you are not one of those who will be found in the chronicles of those who went shipwreck in the faith.

Throw your anchor out. Anchor yourself. Go to God in prayer. Your danger will immediately decrease. The storm will begin to pass you by. You won't be driven so hard by the winds.

Listen to me! The devil will do everything he possibly can to keep you out of prayer. He will do everything from keeping you too busy to making you feel you pray enough already. He will get you stuck on yourself. Before you can realize it, you will be thinking too highly of yourself.

Fall on your face before God and deal with yourself. Repent of all your sins. Purge yourself from your ungodly ways. Admit to yourself who and what you really are. Stop pretending to be something you are not.

If you can't get free from those things that defile you and torment you, go find a friend or a Christian leader to pray with you. If you put effort into it, God will surely bring it to pass. Draw nigh unto Him; He'll draw nigh unto you.

CHAPTER 5

GOD'S WORD – AN ANCHOR TO THE SOUL

"Let us hold fast the profession of our faith without wavering; (for he is faithful that promised;)

And let us consider one another to provoke unto love and to good works:

Not forsaking the assembling of ourselves together, as the manner of some is; but exhorting one another: and so much the more, as ye see the day approaching.

For if we sin wilfully after that we have received the knowledge of the truth, there remaineth no more sacrifice for sins."

Hebrews 10:23-26

18

HOW TO AVOID SHIPWRECK

"... I have found the book of the law in the house of the Lord ..."

2 Kings 22:8

Go to church! This is where you are going to find the richest portion of the Word of God. Church is where you practice fellowship among the believers. Corporate worship and teamwork take place when we come together. The pastor is there and has a message that is for you. It is from God for you. Take your family, and assemble yourselves with other believers under the government of your pastor.

People who don't go to the house of the Lord on a consistent basis are only fooling themselves. They are going shipwreck. You cannot make it without Bible teaching, fellowship and Christian governments. You cannot make it!

Many people have been caught away from the church assembly. They say there are no good pastors and there are no good churches. They are wrong. I feel sorry for them. They are so deceived.

People all over America are meeting in cellars and attics and garages and barns. Do you know why? Well, I tell you this – it isn't because there is a shortage of church families or pastors.

Most of these people have rejected the truth. They have rejected good leadership. They are deceived. They think they can choose each other to be the pastor or teacher or prophet of the group. They are foolish. They are headed for a horrible, disastrous shipwreck. We will all hear of it. We will all witness it. What a shame!

Now, listen! You do not have to crash. You can change. Don't let the storms of life do you in.

Throw your anchor overboard and stabilize your vessel. You must take immediate action. You must stop your life from being blown all about by the winds.

Read your Bible at home. Listen to preaching and teaching on cassette tapes, radio and television. Get all of the Word of God that you can. You can never get too much.

Go to church. Enjoy your pastor's ministry. Take your Bible with you and take notes. This will be a large step in anchoring your life in Jesus.

Stop praying to get delivered from the storm. Prepare yourself to make it through successfully. Don't you know there will be other storms of life? Jesus didn't pray for His disciples to be delivered from the world, but rather that they would "overcome" it. This is what we must do – overcome those horrible storms of life by anchoring and stabilizing ourselves in the Word of God.

Go buy yourself a Bible translation that you can understand. Find a version that fits you. You can always change later in your Christian walk. It is very important for you to be able to understand what you read when you open the Book.

Go buy a video or two or perhaps an audio-cassette series that teaches Bible principles that apply to your daily situations. This will not only keep you in the Word, but it will give you a variety of ministry.

Make the Word of God a priority in your life. Give yourself to study, and God will honor you and calm the storms of life that rage against you.

CHAPTER 6

GOD'S MONEY – AN ANCHOR TO THE SOUL

"Woe unto you, scribes and Pharisees, hypo-crites! for ye pay tithe of mint and anise and cummin, and have omitted the weightier matters of the law, judgment, mercy, and faith: these ought ye to have done, and not to leave the other undone."

Matthew 23:23

"And verily they that are of the sons of Levi, who receive the office of the priesthood, have a commandment to take tithes of the people according to the law, that is, of their brethren, though they come out of the loins of Abraham."

Hebrews 7:5

21

"Bring ye all the tithes into the storehouse, that there may be meat in mine house, and prove me now herewith, saith the Lord of hosts, if I will not open you the windows of heaven, and pour you out a blessing, that there shall not be room enough to receive it."

Malachi 3:10

"No man can serve two masters: for either he will hate the one, and love the other; or else he will hold to the one, and despise the other. Ye cannot serve God and mammon."

Matthew 6:24

"For the love of money is the root of all evil: which while some coveted after, they have erred from the faith, and pierced themselves through with many sorrows."

1 Timothy 6:10

I believe more people have left churches and cursed pastors because of money than for any other single reason. Of course, their hearts aren't right to begin with, or they wouldn't curse, they wouldn't leave and they wouldn't be so bothered.

Money! All of us have to come to the place where we are not going to serve it, and it isn't going to stop us from serving Jesus.

Jesus taught us that our hearts would be wherever our treasures were. A great way to insure you will always have a heart for the Gospel is to invest your belongings and treasures in the Gospel.

HOW TO AVOID SHIPWRECK

Every believer has to deal with this issue. God's portion is God's portion. Steal it if you want to, but it's still God's. Steal it, borrow it and call it anything you want to, but it is still God's! Don't get caught in a storm of life with God's money in your pocket. This is dangerous!

More people miss church services and prayer meetings because of money than probably anything else. They have to work overtime or on Sundays or extra days in order to keep their jobs and pay their bills. Isn't it disgusting that people will listen and obey their employers over their God? They will put hours and days into work for money, but the Sunday sermon had better not go overtime!

The percentage of livelihood that most people give to the work of the Lord is shameful. They have their cottages, vacations, sports and toys and, of course, all of the up-to-date electronics in their homes, but they are just about bankrupt in the Kingdom account.

These people are on Death Row. They are soon going to wither and be no more. Why? They are wallowing in worldly goods and denying Gospel responsibility. They are going to go shipwreck if they don't rescue themselves.

You and I have to decide each day to keep money lower than the Kingdom of God. The world we live in is a money-oriented world. We must not conform to it but be transformed by the renewing of our minds. (Read Romans 12:1-2.)

Where are you at with money? Do you hoard it up? Are you stingy? Do you spend more on yourself than what is right? Do you cheat on your tithe? Do you turn your head from the poor? Do you neglect to give to missions? Are you working so much overtime that it robs you from church? Do you use your church time to run to your cottage, or play with your favorite toy or participate in your favorite sport? Do you judge your pastor, and are you suspicious of how the offerings are disbursed?

If you answered "yes" to any of the above, you are about to suffer shipwreck. You are wrong, and your priorities are wrong.

Preachers are not exempt! A grave, awesome accountability will rest upon those who are recruiting speaking appointments for money. The same is true of those who only go to the "big-offering" churches.

Get your heart right about money. Use it properly. Give God more than His portion. Quit worrying about your needs. Quit following after your own desires. Anchor your soul and avoid financial shipwreck. Be a faithful steward and get all your money matters in the proper priority. You will feel good about it, and it will stabilize your life considerably.

This is a very serious problem. We can't afford to ignore it. We can't afford to allow it to grow. We must work hard to get our heads and money separated, and our hearts and money together. Your heart will correctly guide you about expenditures, tithing, giving and stewardship.

Believe God to discipline you and give you the wisdom to do well in your dealings with mammon.

CHAPTER 7

CONSISTENCY – AN ANCHOR
TO THE SOUL

*"Cast not away therefore your confidence,
which hath great recompense of reward."*

Hebrews 10:35

*"...and that he is a rewarder of them that
diligently seek him."*

Hebrews 11:6

*"And let us not be weary in well doing: for in
due season we shall reap, if we faint not."*

Galatians 6:9

*"Thou therefore endure hardness, as a good
soldier of Jesus Christ.*

*No man that warreth entangleth himself with
the affairs of this life; ..."*

2 Timothy 2:3-4

The word is ... don't quit! Don't throw away the confidence you have. Don't let your heart be troubled. David explained his steadfastness this way:

> *"... my expectation is from him.*
>
> *He only is my rock and my salvation: he is my defence; I shall not be moved."*
>
> Psalm 62:5-6
>
> *"He shall not be afraid of evil tidings: his heart is fixed, trusting in the Lord."*
>
> Psalm 112:7

This must also be us if we are going to stand and not fall. We must be steadfast and strong in the Lord. I don't know why Christians want to quit so easily. It seems like so many of them have little or no endurance! They want to cry, complain and fold under the least little bit of hardship or suffering.

People seem to have such a hard time staying in one place for any real amount of time. They seem to want to run here and there, chasing some rainbow or some dream. Many Christians just can't seem to be faithful in their duties. They are zealous for a while but soon tire out.

Lately, I've had to block my ears from so many Christians' speech. They voice how tired they are and how they need to rest and vacation and take time off. Many are just going home and abandoning the work of the Lord. "Burned out," they say. I say they are quitters! No backbone! Lazy! Uninterested!

We've got to be strong in the Lord. We've got to dig in and get the work of the Lord done. Whether it is easy or hard;

whether it takes a short time or a long time; whether it costs a little money or a lot; whether we like it or not.

We don't have the right to just quit and go home. We don't have the right to abandon God's work and go about our merry way.

People say that they are called to do something different. They claim that God called them away, that God directed them to defect or quit. Wrong! They are confused. God encourages us and fortifies us to go on. He supplies and empowers us to win!

I'm concerned about Christians who obtain a passive, brow-beaten, quitting attitude. I don't think they are going to make it at all. I know they are in trouble. The devil is monitoring their lives, and he is about to take them captive.

These sobbing, sniveling, crying, self-pitying, quitting saints are about to go severely shipwreck in the faith. Lord, have mercy!

Stand up! Shake yourself! Slap yourself! Cast off that old fleshly, pitiful sorrow! Pick up your chin and march on! Pick up your sickle, thrust it in and reap! Pick up your family members and go to church!

You must form good, Christian habits and then stick with them. Base them on the truth and make them an integral, consistent part of your life! If you have to, take only one area at a time and force yourself to do it time and time again.

Go to church, pray, read your Bible, get your tithes in, stir up your zeal – and do it consistently. It will save you from horrible shipwreck.

If you have to, find a friend that respects you and delegate to them the job of pushing and provoking you to good works. If you knew you were going to be rebuked by this friend every time you stayed home from church, made a bad confession, misused money or voiced weariness and sluggish attitudes, you would be much more attentive to be faithful.

Hezekiah leaned on his faithfulness when he was told to get ready for his own funeral. He went to God and made mention of his consistent, faithful service to his God. God honored him and healed him. Would God do the same for you? Yes – if you had enough consistency in your service record to lean on.

Please don't grow lazy. Keep oil in your lamp. Keep your fire burning. Don't become a sluggard who slowly backs out of everything until you are known as a backslider or a quitter.

I will be believing with you that you will rebuke your flesh and go hard after God. You **can** finish your course and keep the faith! Others have.

AVOIDING SHIPWRECK

ANCHOR YOUR SOUL IN JESUS

FOUR GREAT ANCHORS

- PURGE YOURSELF THROUGH PRAYER

- GO TO CHURCH – GET THE WORD

- GET YOUR HEART RIGHT ABOUT MONEY

- BE CONSISTENT – DON'T QUIT

CONCLUSION

YOU CAN BE SAVED FROM ETERNAL DAMNA-TION and get God's help now in this life. All you have to do is humble your heart, believe in Christ's work at Calvary for you, and pray the prayer below.

"Dear Heavenly Father:

I know that I have sinned and fallen short of Your expectations of me. I have come to realize that I cannot run my own life. I do not want to continue the way I've been living, neither do I want to face an eternity of torment and damnation.

I know that the wages of sin is death, but I can be spared from this through the gift of the Lord Jesus Christ. I believe that He died for me, and I receive His provision now. I will not be ashamed of Him, and I will tell all my friends and family members that I have made this wonderful decision.

Dear Lord Jesus:

Come into my heart now and live in me and be my Savior, Master and Lord. I will do my very best to chase after You and to learn your ways by submitting to a pastor, reading my Bible, going to a church that preaches about **You** and keeping sin out of my life.

I also ask You to give me the power to be healed from any sickness and disease and to deliver me from those things that have me bound.

I love You and thank You for having me, and I am eagerly looking forward to a long, beautiful relationship with You."

Other Books by Mark T. Barclay

Building A Supernatural Church
A step-by-step guide to pioneering, organizing, and establishing a local church.

Charging The Year 2000
This book will alert you and bring your attention to the many snares and falsehoods that Satan will try to deceive and seduce last-day believers with.

Enduring Hardness
A must for every believer's library. You will have the roar of a lion and the accomplishments of the Apostle Paul.

How To Avoid Shipwreck
A book of preventive medicine helping people stay strong and full of faith. You will be strengthened by this book.

How To Relate To Your Pastor
It is very important in these last days that God's people understand the office of Pastor. As we put into practice these principles, the church will grow in numbers, and also increase its vision for the world.

Improving Your Performance
Every leader everywhere needs to read this book. It will help tremendously in the organization and unity of your ministry and working force.

Preachers Of Righteousness
As you read this book, you will be both edified and challenged to not only do the work of the ministry, but also do it with humility, honesty, and godliness.

Seducing Spirits
This is not a book on demonology. It is a book about people who are close to being in trouble with God because of demon activity or fleshly bad attitudes.

Sheep-Goats-Wolves
A scriptural yet practical explanation of human behavior in our local churches and how church leaders and members can deal with each other.

The Sin Of Familiarity
This book is a scriptural study on the most devastating sin in the Body of Christ today. The truths in this book will make you aware of this excess familiarity and reveal to you some counterattacks.

The Sin Of Lawlessness
Lawlessness always challenges authority, and ultimately is designed to hurt people. This book will convict those who are in lawlessness, and warn those who could be furture victims. It will help your life, and straighten your walk with Him.

The Remnant
God has always had a people and will always have a people. Dr. Barclay speaks of the upcoming revival and how we can be part of God's remnant.

What About Death?
A book that is bringing great understanding to the scriptural teaching on the death of loved ones, as well as eternal citizenship.

Videos

• **Seven Bible Ways To Properly Relate To Your Pastor**

• **Seduction & Deception**

• **The Remnant Church**

To receive Dr. Barclay's bimonthly publication and receive a complete listing of books and audio tapes (singles and series) available, contact us at the address below.

MARK BARCLAY PUBLICATIONS
P.O. BOX 588
MIDLAND, MI 48640
(517) 835-3297